MIAMI TRAVEL GUIDE FOR WOMEN

For Women, by Women: The Insider's Guide to the "Gateway to the Americas"

By Erica Stewart

Published by:

ALEX-PUBLISHING

Note from the Author:

Welcome to Miami...Bienvenidos a Miami!

Miami, at Florida's southeastern tip, is a vibrant city where Cuban influence is infused in every single brick, corner stone, grain of sand and bite of food. What was once the swanky mecca of the rich and famous in the USA has now become one of the most vibrant, multicultural, exotic and fresh party hubs in the whole country. For women travelers, Miami spells FUN, SUN, SURF, SHOPPING and SENSATIONAL feasting, so if you're in the hunt for a rewarding and unique beach-side escapade, then you could pick no better place.

Let us guide you through the maze of this amazing holiday destination and let us help you discover why Miami is rated so highly by all those who have come before you. From the nightlife, to the eating out, the shopping, the sightseeing and the blissfully relaxing, you've got the best of Miami right at your fingertips.

ERICA STEWART

Chapter Index

7

Chapter 1: What to know before you go

Romance and party aside, Miami really is quite a unique place to visit, for many varied reason. Exotic yet familiar, busy and chilled out, it embodies the best of north and south American cultures in one stunning hot-spot. Yet it also boasts quite a few peculiarities, so get in the know before you go...and you'll be ready!

Miami is HUGE!

One of the top 10 most populated metropolitan areas in the whole of the USA, Miami stretches more than 180 km (110 miles) north to south, and up to 30 km (20 miles) east to west. Although Downtown and the beaches are the most famous and visited sights, Miami also boasts some amazing day-trip destinations worth checking out if you have more time. Yes, there's more to Miami than sunbathing, shopping and clubbing...who knew? Take a daytrip to the stunning

Everglades National Park, take a glass-bottom boat tour through the third largest reef system in the world or enjoy a superb day trip driving through the gorgeous islands of the Florida Keys.

It's oh-so Latino

Visiting Miami is like taking a trip to Cuba, minus the extra stamp in your passport. This city is home to the largest population of Spanish speakers outside of Latin America, so although English is obviously the official language, it would help to know a bit of Espanol. Yet the influence of southerly neighbors doesn't just end with the language. Everything here sort of runs on Cuban rime too, so if you expect the bus to be there at 10.30 am. or that show to start at 8 pm on the dot...well...it won't! Moreover, life here works on Latin American time as well: dinner's at 9 pm, clubbing only starts at midnight and heading home at 5 am constitutes an 'early night'.

Watch your stuff

Beware of your belongings in crowded places – especially Miami Beach – as petty theft (of purses/cell phones) is quite prevalent.

Top it off!

Topless sunbathing is perfectly legal here, although in very central beaches, frequented by local families, it's considered very poor form. If you do want to shed the extra layer then head to the beaches along 17th street. Want to take it *all* off and get an even tan? Then the nude bathing spot of Haulover Beach is for you.

Want to spend less? Stay in Fort Lauderdale

Fort Lauderdale is only a half hour bus ride north of Miami and if you don't mind the commute it actually makes for a great – and much cheaper – base. It's also an excellent day trip destination for food, shopping and sightseeing, and beaches in Fort Lauderdale are much less crowded then those in Miami.

Miami is all about variety

Off the west coast of Miami you'll find Naples, a luxurious retirement destination renowned for its pristine beaches and super luxe waterfront properties. Nature lovers in Miami can pick from beach or park reprieves, with plenty on offer. The city boasts quite a few stunning parks, ideal for a jog or picnic. Miami is undergoing a transition of sorts, from hip and at times trashy beach hub to sophisticated arty capital. Luckily, if you visit now, you can experience both sides!

Catch a festival

Thanks to the multi-cultural essence of Miami, the city boasts many cultural festivals, of different flavors, all year long.

Mind the extra charges

When dining out, especially at any of the beachside eateries, do note that service and 'beach' tax are often added to the bill. Enquire beforehand so you know what to expect.

Rent a car

Feeling really adventurous? Rent a car! This is, by far, the best way to see the best of Miami (beaches, shopping, nightlife) as the city is not nearly as well serviced, by public transport, as one would expect. Not only will you have priceless independence but you also save a lot on pricey taxi fares and waste much less time than you would when using public transport. Traffic can be a nightmare, but if you time it right, it's definitely a doable option.

Miami beauties – not always au naturel

Could everyone *really* be *that* perfect?! In Miami, yes, they can. Maybe it's genetic, maybe it's hard work, or maybe it's plastic surgery. Who knows? Fact is, a holiday to Miami has the potential to make any woman feel...less than perfect. Be prepared for the onslaught of physical perfection on show, and enjoy the eye candy!

Air-conditioning. It's an obsession

Pack one light sweater, for that night at the movies or that shopping mall that's air-conditioned to feel like Antarctica.

Best time to visit

Miami, thanks to its latitude, enjoys mainly just two seasons: warm and dry, or hot and wet. The northern Spring, between the months of May and June, is arguably the best time to visit as you'll find the temps manageable and the rain fairly inexistent. Frugal travelers who want to take advantage of great savings should head here in Summer (July – September) however heavy downpours and sweltering heat – with its accompanying humidity – can present issues for some.

Stay safe

Safety is not a huge issue in Miami, as long as you stay away from Overtown and Liberty City, as well as Downtown of an evening. The latter, should be noted, is more 'sketchy' rather than dangerous, so if you're an experienced female traveler you still should not run into any problems. The beachside suburbs are the busiest and safest of all.

Nevertheless, it pays to never be too relaxed when travelling, especially as a solo woman. Leave all your valuables at home, choose a hotel in a well-lit and busy area and don't indulge in big boozy nights in a foreign city, on your own. These three very basic actions ought to ensure you have a fantastic and hassle-free time in Miami.

Choose the right place

Even if in Miami for just a couple of nights, and think you'll only be in your hotel to rest your weary head, it pays to spend some time picking the right place. It should be safe, comfortable, well rated and in a good area. Ask friends and family for recommendation and check out blogs of women your age/status to ascertain what their previous experiences have been, and if they liked where they stayed.

Have a back-up plan

Plan to arrive during the day, at least 3 hours before sunset, to ensure you not reach your hotel in the dark. Have an alternative plan and hotel ready, in case you arrive and find the place/district not to your liking. Trust your instincts and opt to lose a cancellation fee if need be. If it doesn't 'feel right' it probably isn't. Have a back-up plan just in case.

Keep an open mind

Plastic is everywhere (on people's bums, lips and most souvenirs) yet if you go with an open mind you can have an excellent time. Miami is like a Latino version of Vegas and as long as you know that to begin with, you won't be caught out by all the glitz, glamour and at times, even tackiness. But in the midst of it, with all the wonderful art and amazing one-off boutiques, there are plenty of hidden gems to be discovered.

Buy a beach-brolly. Seriously

If you're planning on lying on the beach all day every day of your vacation, the smart thing to do is to actually buy a beach umbrella on your first day. Stay just three days and it'll cost less than a three-day rental. Before leaving, simply donate or sell it back to a new guest at your hotel.

Best views are free

For a superlative sunset view of Miami's cityscape, head to the front gardens of the Miami Children's Museum. It's right here.

Choose the best of two evils

Beachside eateries are overpriced, that's a given, but if you want to pay just a little less, opt for Miami Beach over South Beach.

General safety tips

Alone or with friends, Miami is generally a safe place to visit for women, especially as most out-of-towners will tend to converge around SoBe and Miami Beach. Still, some common sense and a few good tips ought to really ensure all the stories you come home with, will be good ones!

- Renting a car? Don't leave any valuables in sight and if using a rented GPS, remove it from the windscreen and wipe away the mark left by the suction cap. Thieves are known to look for this.

- Don't flash any expensive jewelry, watch or purse around and never, EVER leave your belongings unattended at the beach when you go for a swim.

- Don't walk down dark alleys or deserted streets, even if it means taking a longer route to where you need to go.

- If travelling with girlfriends, stick together in clubs and don't leave your drink unattended, or accept a drink from a stranger, unless you've taken it directly from the barman who made it.

- Make sure your hotel room has a safe and lock up your valuables at all times. Staying in for the evening? Lock the door.

- Taxis may be expensive but at 3 am they're still the safest way to get home.

- Every bad vacation story starts with 'so then we had another drink...' Keep the alcohol consumption in check when in Miami!

- Your biggest danger in Miami? Being run over when you cross the road. Seriously. No-one's looking where they're going, and that seems to include those behind the wheel of their car. Watch out.

- Hailing from abroad? The emergency number in Miami is 911. Jot it down and keep it both on paper and on your phone. If you do need it, you'll be in a stressful situation and you probably won't remember it.

ERICA STEWART

Chapter 2: Getting in & general overview

Getting In

As a busy and coveted tourist hub, Miami is easy to reach by car, plane or bus, from anywhere in the country and beyond.

BY AIR

Miami's International Airport is one of the busiest, and arguably most disorganized, in off of North America. When arriving or leaving, factor in at least an extra hour or two. This is the main hub for American Airlines, which connects this Florida city to all major capitals the world over. Many International carriers also service flights to this airport.

There are free shuttles which connect passengers to the MetroRail and TriRail stations and, from here, you can connect to certain areas of Miami by bus, monorail or train. Renting a car is incredibly popular here, as stated in the precious chapter, due to the lack of a continuous public transport system. Hopping between trains and buses can be very time consuming.

If staying in Miami Beach, take the Airprot Flyer Bus instead. Think you'll use public transport here? Then purchase your EASY Card at the airport, to save on some serious cash. For more details, refer to our 'Getting Around' chapter.

The Fort Lauderdale International Airport is not nearly as chaotic as Miami's and checking in and out is much faster. It is serviced by many low-cost carriers, however do note that the distance from Downtown and the Miami Beach almost negates the time saved, so it's a bit of a hit and miss. There is a free shuttle which connects you to the Miami Airport rail stations and, from here, use the above-mentioned options to get to your hotel.

BY TRAIN

The trek to Miami by train from New York is long and arduous, yet it can be done in about 24 hours. Services are offered to their major cities along the eastern seaboard. Check out Amtrak for more details on routes, timetables and ticket prices.

BY COACH

Long-haul bus services to Miami are offered from Orlando, Tampa and other Florida points, as well as other cities in Florida, Georgia and other states. Greyhound, Gray Line and Red Coach are just some of the most popular.

General Overview of Miami

There's much more to Miami than South Beach, although many visitors would argue otherwise. This sprawling city is chock-full of attractive, vibrant districts just itching to be explored. Want to be a traveler and not a tourist? Then get to know all of Miami's stunning district and decide which one's best for you.

Open up this handy map of Miami and follow our lead as we guide you through the city's most popular hoods. Of course, the world is your oyster and you can indeed stay anywhere you like. Even Fort Lauderdale if you don't mind the daily commute!

EAST - Miami & South Beach

Sure, there may be more to Miami than just its sparkling beaches...but that's always a great place to start, right? You don't get more iconic Miami than seaside Ocean Drive, and the Strip (aka Collins Ave) brimming with its colorful ArtDeco hotels makes for a stunning scenery. The 6 mile long Boardwalk is the heart of the action and a bubbling hive of joggers, walkers, designer shoppers and show-offers. Just a step north is Hollywood Beach which is much quieter and more sedate, if that's your thing. This whole seaside stretch is the second most expensive area to stay in Miami, and by far the best people-watching spot.

Are you a Miami beach-style woman? Why not stay here and find out?!

CENTRAL - Downtown Miami

Downtown is Miami's business district, which boasts quite a few hotels and an infinite amount of great shopping. The cityscape really is very beautiful and, if you're going to not stay on a beach then this would definitely be an excellent second choice. However, do note that after dark, downtown is neither hip and happening, nor is it all that safe, so if you're a lone female traveler, who likes to take an evening stroll, this may not be the best place in which to stay.

WEST – Little Havana

Little Havana, just to the west, is home to the best Cuban cigar shopping in town, and a myriad of trendy little eateries and boutiques. If you've always dreamed of visiting Havana, but never got the chance, this may be your best bet yet. Vibrant evening scenes and cheap but excellent food are probably Little Havana's biggest draws.

SOUTH – The Gables and The Grove

Coconut Grove and Coral Gables are two very affluent districts of Miami, renowned for their luxury villas, resorts and premier shopping malls. Commercially, these areas are kicking butt all over Miami, however the gentrification has kept all the arty types, which used to hang around here in the 70s, well out of its boundaries. Neverthelesss, plenty of uni students keep the streets buzzing at night, so this is still a super fun place to stay if you're a young, adventurous woman.

SOUTHEAST – Key Biscayne

Key Biscayne is connected to Coral Gables via a long Causeway, and is home to the popular Miami Seaquarium and fantastic water sport beaches. Insanely different to its northern seaside cousins, Key Biscayne is very expensive, very exclusive but also very secluded and utterly peaceful.

Chapter 3: How to get around

If you've managed to make it out of the Miami Airport with your sanity intact, then kudos to you! The good news is that getting around Miami is infinitely easier than navigating the airport, although the bad news is that not by all *that* much. Of course, your transport missions would be helped greatly if you are able to stay in whichever area you think you'll be spending most time in.

On foot or bicycle

If staying in Miami Beach or Downtown, then getting around on foot, or on handy rental CityBikes (the latter with convenient pick-up and drop-off at various locations) is the best way to go. Cycling along the Boardwalk, of course, is a very popular and infinitely beautiful pastime here. Simply sign up to the program, show up at a station, rent a bike and off you go.

Download this handy map of bike rental stations all over Miami.

By rental car

When we said you should seriously consider renting a car, of course we meant to get out and see Miami's neighboring wonders. In the city centre, you'll find traffic to be chaotic at best, thanks to the continuous 'upgrades' which seem to go on forever. Parking can also be quite expensive, especially own by the beach. It's a great idea to rent a car at the airport if you're planning to spend the first few days taking day trips, and the rest of the time chilling out in Miami. Alternatively, head to your hotel with public transport and rent a car in the city after a few days to get out and explore the wonderful attractions nearby.

By free Metromover

Downtown is serviced by the free Metromover, which connects to Metrorail at Government Centre and Brickell. For short bunny hops in town, this is just ideal.

You can take a load off your legs and enjoy great cityscape views along the ride. There are 21 stations along the route, roughly one for every two city blocks. You can print your map right here.

By SoBe Local

For mysterious reasons, the convenient SoBe (for South Beah) Local bus seems to be overlooked by many visitors, which is a true travesty. The comprehensive loop of South Beach, new and air-conditioned buses and cheap-as-chips ticket prices (25 cents!) make the SoBe Local Bus the best way to get about in this area. Buses run every 10-15 minutes every day, starting at 7.45 am on weekdays and 10 am on weekends. Services cease at 1 am.

By bus

Buses service the whole Miami metropolitan area and although getting the hang of this extensive system may not be worthwhile, for just a few days, it is imperative if staying for a week or more. Check out the Miami transit page for routes and timetables.

By MetroRail

Miami's MetroRail is a fast, easy and affordable way to get around the city, although the dual-line system is not nearly as extensive, as perhaps it could be. You can reach the city from the airport this way, as well as many museums, points of interests and many of the city's parks. While the rail doesn't operate at night, a nightbus schedule picks up the slack, essentially providing convenient transport 24 hours a day.

Passes and multi-day cards

Whether travelling by MetroBus or MetroRail, get yourself an EASY Card, which can be easily topped up, and will save you quite a bit on individual fare tickets. Download this Transit Tracker app on your i-phone or i-pad and have all the details of Miami's public transport, right at your fingertips when you need them most.

By Taxi

Sure, taxi riding around town may set you back a bit but there's really no more convenient way to navigate Miami. Do note that while in peak hour you'll be able to hail one down with ease – although only legally outside train station - you may need to call ahead for off-time travel. Yellow Cab and Central Cab are the two most popular companies, in downtown and Miami Beach, respectively. Use this fare calculator to estimate travel costs.

By Hop-on/hop-off bus

The popular hop-on/hop-off service in Miami is certainly not every woman's cup of tea, yet it does offer some great benefits. Anyone who is in Miami for a single day, or two at most, can certainly make great use of this bus. Like to be organized? Then hop[on for a full loop to get your bearings and note the points which would interest you most, and make a list of things to see and do. There are 20 stops in total, commentary in several languages and frequent bus services. Tickets can include hotel pick-up and drop-off too.

By organized tour

Organized tours are actually a great way to 'get around' Miami, all the while discovering all there is to know about this enticing city. Here are the best tours in town, ideal for you to join on your first day in Miami.

Miami Culinary Tours – Eat your way through Miami and discover all the culinary secrets of Little Havana and all other areas of the city.

Everglades Adventure Tours – take an unforgettable airboat ride through the protected Everglades and you'll get to experience the most natural, wild and amazing side of Florida.

Speedboat Tours – Because seeing Miami at breakneck speed is totally AWESOME!

Flyboard – It's fun, it's crazy and it's got Miami written all over it. Channel your inner dolphin and fly high above the waves. Watch your landings!

E-bicycle Tour: Explore Miami on two wheels for 2 hours or a full day. Rent your bikes and have them delivered to your hotel, or let one of the knowledgeable guides show you around.

Chapter 4: Top 10 iconic Miami experiences

Hit South Beach

Whether you're a surfer, rollerblader, cyclist, bikini stroller or just humble sunbather, South Beach is bound to be your first port of call when visiting Miami. There is something about the aquamarine waters, sparkling sand and stylish Ocean Drive that make this the most popular spot in town. Shop for designer gear in the up-market boutiques, rub shoulders with the rich and famous in one of the many trendy cafés or spend an entire day in one of the über-luxe beach clubs. Feeling energized? Then surf some wave, learn to paddle board, join a volleyball match or sunset yoga class. In Miami, you can do all these things, and more.

Admire the ArtDeco architecture

South Beach was THE hot spot in the 30s and 40s and although that particular golden era is well and truly in the past, there are still plenty of architectural influences to admire, along Ocean Drive. The colorful, eccentric façades of over 800 buildings make up the Art Deco District and are, aside the beach and its gorgeous people, the most photogenic subjects in South Beach. Pick up an audio guide from the Welcome Centre on 1001 Ocean Drive

Visit the Vizacaya Museum & Gardens

The Vizcaya is Miami's premier wedding reception venue and all you need do is to take one look at it to understand why that would be. Built by a filthy rich industrialist in the early 1900s, this incredible palace is as opulent on the inside as it is on the outside. This is the most eye-catching sight on Biscayne Bay, and that's saying a lot. The lovely gardens are a tranquil reprieve from the hustle of the bay, yet touring Vizcaya's interior is the true highlight. Come to Miami to admire period European treasures? Well why on earth not?!

Get lost in Little Havana

The flood of Cubans which engulfed Miami in the 60s, after Castro came to power, permanently changed the essence of this city, in every way imaginable. Little Havana, just to the west of Downtown, is what was born out of that colossal Latin influx and, in many ways, is the most enticing corner in Miami. Nowadays, Little Havana is not only home to Cubans, by many other Latin American immigrants, making it a multi-cultural hive like no other. Here, you'll find amazing hidden art galleries, produce and food markets, cigar and rum shops, arts and craft stores and ever-vibrant street scenes. From street murals to blaring music, this district, and the main Calle Ocho in particular, have the knack for kidnapping visitors for days on end. You'll find a very useful Visitor Centre on 1600 Calle Ocho (SW 8th Street), where you can get info and buy some great souvenirs. On a safety point of note: although this area is much safer than it has ever been, wandering the dark alleyways, late at night, is still ill-advised for tourists, most especially women travelers.

Soar high on a sunrise balloon ride

There are few things in life, which are as magical as seeing the sun rise from a vertiginous height, aboard a hot-air balloon. Soaring high above Miami, and admiring the spectacular coastline, cityscape, Everglades and Pacific Ocean from the air is one of the most bucket-list worthy activities you could ever indulge in. At $250 a pop, flights don't come cheap, but are sure to be utterly unforgettable. Just take a sneaky peek at the pics on Balloon Miami's website and you'll be sold!

Attend a festival

Visit Miami at any time and you may be forgiven for thinking this is one of the most happening places in all of the US. It really is. The yearly events calendar is chock full of cultural events, food fiestas, concerts, open air theatres, sporting events and more. Simply enter the dates you wish to visit on the online calendar search and see what will be happening in and around Miami.

Take an airboat through the Everglades

The Everglades are the US' largest tropical wilderness and a UNESCO-listed protected wetlands. The park is a priceless breeding ground for countless animals, and although waters have been receding in recent years, it's still an utterly breathtaking place to visit. From Miami, you can visit on a boat tour, the most popular two being Airboat in Everglades and Buffalo Tigers. See authentic tribal dwellings and scour the waters for creatures you'd be happy not to get too close to!

Watch a Miami Heat game

Miami's most beloved basketball team is an obsession in these parts and watching a live game at the American Airlines Arena during your visit, is bound to be one of the most memorable cultural experiences of all. You can check out the game schedule and buy tickets online at the NBA official website.

Shop 'till you drop

You certainly won't be short for places to shop in Miami, but if you're short on time, or wish to just spend a whole day in one single spot, then head to the Lincoln Road Mall, the swankiest shopping strip in town and stiff competitor to Ocean Drive, albeit for different reasons. This relaxing yet busy pedestrian outdoor mall stretches west to east, between 17th and 17th streets, and brims at the rim with excellent boutiques, trendy cafés, restaurants, museums and even malls-within-malls. Among the many stores are Macy's, Victoria's Secret, Gucci, Gao, Lacoste and a host of other well-known brands.

Discover Little Haiti

Colorful, vibrant and offering a great insight into Haitian culture, Little Haiti has been a thriving nook of Miami for well over four decades. Over the past decade, however, a heady dose of gentrification has changed this suburb somewhat, which is not necessarily a negative thing. Once strife with petty – and even larger – crime, Little Haiti is becoming increasingly popular with visitors, although we assume it'll be a few years yet before it reaches the popularity of Little Havana.

Chapter 5: Miami's best landmarks

While you're out and about experiencing the best of Miami, make a point to visit the most popular landmarks in town.

Jungle Island

Spread out over 22 acres, Jungle Island is described as an 'interactive zoological park' where visitors can get close and personal with creatures of all size, big and small. If you're an animal lover, then don't miss your chance to visit one of the oldest and most popular tourist attractions in all of Miami. With spectacular views and a wide array of exotic animals, including Australian kangaroos and African penguins among many others, Jungle Island makes for a fun few hours and a is a great alternative to yet 'another day at the beach'. Our only advice is to skip visiting on a Sunday or at any time during eth school holidays. The fun but kitsch animal shows are a magnet for families with children, so the zoo can feel quite crowded on those days.

Miami Zoo

Want to see more wildlife? Then how about Andean condors, Komodo dragons and more African savannah animals then you'd ever see on safari? Zoo Miami is not only the oldest animal park in Florida, but is also the only tropical zoo in all of the United States. The exhibits are top notch and the delightful (air conditioned!) monorail makes getting around eth huge complex very easy. Nevertheless, plan on lots of walking here so wear comfortable shoes. If you're wavering between the zoo and Jungle Island, and only have time to visit one animal sanctuary, then we'd say this one comes up ahead.

Wynwood Art Walk

If you're an art-lover you'll love taking a relaxing an insightful stroll through the Wynwood Art Walk, while learning all about the striking street art along the way.

There are galleries to visit and really cool little cafés as well. Take a group tour, given every Friday and Saturday, to make the most out of your visit.

Museum of Science

Miami's Museum of Science may be closed for renovations until summer 2016, but when it opens in its new location in Museum Park, it's bound to rise up again among the top contenders for the city's best attractions. The new and improved museum is set to be a 'scientific wonderland' with exciting interactive exhibits, a planetarium, aquarium and plenty of education facilities. Watch this space and keep this tip in mind if planning to visit later next year.

Fairchild Tropical Botanic Garden

You need not be an avid botanist to appreciate the importance and striking beauty of the Fairchild Tropical Botanic Gardens, found just a 20 minute drive south of Downtown Miami. Initially opened in 1938 by an avid – and affluent - plant collector, the Gardens are home to some of the most exotic plant species from every corner of the globe. Imported and planted species from Africa, Asia and South America make up the great bulk of the flora here, with a stupendous butterfly exhibit, called Wings of the Tropics, being the absolute highlight. From orchids to African Baobab trees, and more than 80 acres of tropical gorgeousness make up this park. The gardens are a natural haven close to the thriving centre, and host amazing festivals on most weekends. Check out the website to see what's on during your visit, but make a point to visit at any rate.

Coral Castle Museum

This utterly unique open-air museum showcases innumerable and quite huge sculptures made from over one ton of coral. As legend go, this one tops the cake: spurred on by a jilted lover and having healed himself from tuberculosis with magnets, an eccentric Latvian sculptor single-handedly carved all the sculptures in the museum. An interesting hour-long excursion, perfect for anyone looking for something a little different. You'll find the Coral Castle Museum just off the S Dixie Highway (1 – corner Biscayne Drive), about a half hour drive south of Downtown.

Jewish Museum of Florida

Housed within the walls of two former synagogues, in a most unassuming part of Miami, The Jewish Museum of Florida recounts the trials and tribulations of the Jewish community in Florida, and Miami in particular. The JMF is a very enlightening museum with various relics and artifacts, and an interesting souvenir shop to boot. Considering the city's not overrun with historical museums, this one's a bit of a treasure for history-lovers.

Freedom Tower

Spend but a few days in Miami and you'll be left with no doubts as to the immense influence the Cuban community has had on this once 'all American' town. If you're interested in learning more about the mass migration in the 1960s, and about the plight of those who wished to escape Cuba at the time, you'd do well to spend an hour or so at the museum of the Freedom Tower. This very symbolic building was initially the printing press of the Miami News, yet from 1957 was used to process and provide basic health care to Cubans refugees arriving in droves. Set for residential redevelopment in the early 2000s, the Freedom Tower cultural and historical importance were finally recognized. Today, it is a museum, cultural centre and educational facility.

Venetian Pool

This Coral Gables public swimming pool was first opened in 1924 and still retains that old-world charm, as long as you don't visit on weekends. An ocean of screaming young kids tend to take the romance away, ever so slightly . The Venetian Pool is stunningly landscaped and, luckily in many ways, limits the entries per day. Get in early to avoid disappointment.

Oleta River State Park

For nature lovers, there's no better escape than the Oleta River State Park, where you can kayak or canoe through pristine mangroves, alongside shores which were first inhabited by natives over 2000 years ago. The park is easily accessible but you will need a rental car for the easy drive up.

Bass Museum of Art

For lovers of contemporary art, The Bass is a heavenly retreat from the chaotic street scenes of Miami Beach, and holds frequent exhibitions at night. A top spot for a bit of culture.

Chapter 6: Tips for a perfect girly weekend in Miami

Miami is a renowned girl's getaway haven and an insanely popular destination for bachelorette parties and girls-only weekend getaways. From great art to fab hopping, delectable food, endless sun-worshiping, excellent pampering and people-watching, this city seems tailor-made for girls looking to have some fun.

Here are some invaluable tips on how to organize the very best girl's weekend in the land of sun, sea and surf.

Book early for a great deal

There are some great hotel deals to be had however all require you book at least 4-6 months in advance. Have a bachelorette to organize? Be all OCD and book in advance and, in high season, you could save a small fortune.

Choose one large suite over several different rooms

Hanging out together with your girlfriends is, at the end of the day, what you'll want to do most of all, and there's nothing like your own 'living room' in which to chill out, talk and share pre-dinner drinks and snacks. To this end, booking a large suite/apartment is a really great option.

Stock up on water, nibblies & alcohol

There are plenty of grocery and liquor stores in South Beach, so you can stock up on some basics and buy a bottle of Campari and lemonade for happy hour celebrations in your room, while you get ready for a night out. Considering cocktails out in clubs can be quite expensive, this is also a great way to have fun, share drinks and not be worried about a head-shinnying bar bill for what is meant to be a very happy hour!

Stay central

If you want to be close to all the daytime and nighttime action (beaches and clubs) then it pays to make sure you are in a central location, especially if there will be more than 3-4 of you. Dealing with expensive taxis or – heaven forbid – public transport in a larger group, late in the evening, will be a nightmare. For this, South Beach will be your best choice.

Make sure your hotel has beach access & a pool

To really maximize your time in the sun, and together, look for a gorgeous hotel with direct beach access and private pool. Sometimes, you may just want to chill out for a few hours away from the crowds, but still lay in the sun and by the water. A hotel pool is just ideal for that!

Beach it early

Head to the beach early in the morning and don't forget to grab an umbrella as it will get unbearably hot at around lunchtime. For lunch, head up to one of the cafés and enjoy your meal wearing only your biking. In Miami, everyone does it and it's totally fun!

Book restaurants in advance

If travelling in a big girly-group, it's almost essential to book your meals out to popular spots, ahead of time. Dinner and swanky Sunday brunches are so popular in Miami, that finding a table for more than two people, at the last minute, is nearly impossible.

Include a spa day

Planning a day of pampering with the girls usually turns out to be the highlight of all Miami weekend getaways, especially as this is usually the last 'treat' of the trip. We'll give you a comprehensive rundown of Miami's best spas in the next chapter

Include at least one splurge

Including a super special splurge treat over the weekend, will certainly ensure your vacation be an ever-memorable one. Along with the breathtaking sunrise balloon ride, you could also charter a yacht for the day or organize a private dinner sunset cruise.

Plan out some itineraries

It may sound crazy, but don't be surprised if you reach the end of your weekend away in Miami, and have 'forgotten' to do something which you'd been planning on. It happens more often than you can imagine! Jotting down some fun day itineraries, or at least a list of activities you'd like for you all to do, will ensure you never lose track of what there is to see and do. It's also worthwhile keeping in mind that shops open till late so it's best to keep the retail-therapy for the evenings, and enjoy the beaches and parks during the daylight hours.

Want to some ideas on fun, flirty and fabulous things to do on your girly weekend? Here you go!

Book a pole-dancing class

Becoming increasingly popular in Miami, pole-dancing classes are renowned for being hard work and ton of fun when taken with friends. Book an afternoon class at SoBe Pole Dance Studio as a surprise for your girlfriends and you're guaranteed to have an awesome fun time in Miami.

Channel your inner drag queen

Lips is a hilarious drag queen club in Fort Lauderdale and although it specializes in bachelorette parties – complete with erotic cake for the bride-to-be – it's a fantastic club for a girly night out. Outlandish performances, great music and friendly host-esses make it an absolute hoot of a club!

Strike a pose

Booking a surprise photo shoot with Terribly Girly is swiftly becoming de rigeur in Miami. The photography team will help you out with everything from make up to hair style and clothing, and set up ingenious from any era you fancy.

Belt out a tune

Karaoke is not just for tone-deaf uni students and Sing Sing Karaoke in SoBe is the kind of classy joint which has even attracted famous performers from all over the world. Still, just in case, belt out a tune in the privacy of your own VIP room and come give Celine Dion a run for her money.

Watch (him) take it off

Male strip clubs have a bit of a seedy reputation all over the world, but in Miami you'll find some truly classy joints which are ideal for a totally fun night out with the ladies. Choose from Hunk-O-Mania or Manhattan Strip Club, renowned for being the best in their game.

Organize a moviethon

Whether it's Friends, Star Trek, Twilight or Melrose Place, every group of female friends will have at least one TV show or movie obsession in common (alright, maybe not Star Trek!) and spending a whole afternoon lying on the floor of your rented suite, drinking champagne and watching re-run episodes, is an incredibly fun and relaxing thing to do. Just check in, find the closest rental shop and happy viewing!

Whodunnit?

Host your own murder mystery dinner or have a team of professionals come right in and show you how it's done. Pick a fun era – like the gangster-filled 1930s – and giggle your way through a night of mystery, laughs and murder. Download your own game here or contact Miami Murder Mystery.

Take a private cooking class

Maybe you're all avid foodies and can think of nothing better than spending a few hours learning to cook, and feasting on, brand new delicious recipes. You've got loads of options in Miami but some of the most popular are Eleanor Hoh's Asian wok extravaganza and Ayesha's fabulous Indian soiree. Do not that most of the five-star restaurants in Miami, especially those found in luxury hotels, can organize a private cooking class for your group.

Giddy up

Whether you're all experienced riders or horse riding virgins, heading out for a gallop is a wonderful way to experience the exhilarating side of Miami. Professionally and fully-equipped ranches can organize your group, no matter the level of experience – or fear! For the best and most popular ranches and equestrian clubs, look right here.

Hit The Basement

Nightclub, ice-skating rink and disco bowling sound like fun? At The Basement, you can do it all under one roof in one fun night out! This is still very much a local's secret so head there pronto before it gets completely overrun with tourists.

Chapter 7: Best day spas in Miami

From the holistic to the opulent and the frugal, Miami has a spa to suit any woman in need of some zen and yang. For ease of reference, we'll categorize them by price, taking the most affordable one-hour massage as relative guideline. Do note that all these spas have a varied menu of decadent treatments so do check them out online before choosing the one that's right for you.

Budget

Just because you want to feel like a million dollars doesn't mean you need always pay top dollar. Want a cheap, cheerful yet gorgeous spa experience in Miami? Then check these babies out!

Scape Spa - SW 128th St, Miami

Once you take a step inside this spa, and check out the massage prices, you may get the urge to double check. 'Value' for money' doesn't even come close to describing the treatments offered at Scape, which currently include a one hour hot-stone massage for only $32. You read that right. The spa is clean, relaxing, quiet and staffed by gorgeous girls who'll sort out every knot in your body.

Oriental Foot Massage & Spa - **SW 72nd St, Miami**

At first glance, this may look like the kind of average spa you'd see in Southeast Asia. The four massage chairs in front of the TV may not seem all that appealing, but bear in mind the private rooms at the back, and superlative skill of the in-house masseuse, and you'll be pleasantly surprised. The pressure points and Thai massages are to die for!

Soothe - **mobile massage!**

How does an affordable mobile massage therapist sound? Perfect, right? The gals at Soothe come fully equipped with everything they need to revitalize your body, right in the comfort of your own hotel room. Professional, safe and incredibly well rated, this mobile spa is ideal if you've just spent the whole day walking around Miami, want a massage but are too exhausted to leave your room. Soothe can arrange a therapist within an hour, and deliver massages up until midnight, 7 days a week!

Mid-range

Nava Med Wellness & Spa - SW 3rd Ave, Miami

The excellent treatments and superlative service is what sets Nava Med apart from the rest of its contemporaries. Relaxing music, nourishing teas, gentle hands and gorgeous products seal the deal. Enjoy a milk and honey pedi, white mud mask and hot oil massage at the end of your Miami vacation and you'll be totally transformed.

Body, Mind, Spirit - Old Dixie H'way, Miami

Dubbed 'Miami's most hidden spa gem', Body, Mind, Spirit boasts a lovely, relaxing ambience and offers a wide range of treatments from the relaxing to the useful. Need a massage and your eyebrows waxed? You can have it all here. Groupon-mania can make getting an appointment here a little lengthy, so book ahead. There are very good reasons this spa is so popular!

Massage Envy Spa - N Miami Avenue

If convenience and a very good pampering session are what you're after, then you'll find it at Massage Envy. Right in Midtown and with a wealth of treatments on offer, including facials and aromatherapy body treatments.

Luxury

When only the best will do...

Lapis Spa – Collins Ave, SoBe

When it comes to opulent pampering, there are few spas which can match the Lapis. Dubbed 'the most beautiful spa in America' this haven of luxury is mind-bogglingly stunning and eye-wateringly expensive – except if you score one of their monthly specials, that is. Book a private suite, which comes with your own private bath butler (we're not kidding) and if you're not feeling rejuvenated and reborn after a mineral soak, sea salt body scrub, detoxifying clay wrap and four-hand massage, then there's a fair chance you're actually dead.

The Palms – Collins Ave, SoBe

This Aveda-dedicated spa boasts poolside cabanas so you can enjoy the two best activities in Miami in swift swoop. This head to toe emporium offers everything from relaxing treatments to torturous ones (need a wax?) and considering you can also have your hair and make-up done just before you leave, you can visit the Palms and literally feel like a new woman!

Trump National Doral Miami – NW 87th Ave, Doral

With 'Trump' in the name, you can pretty much guess that there is nothing understated or 'average' about this spa. The Doral Miami is where the Miss America gals get ready for their pageant and it's a place you may just want to get lost in. Forever. With gorgeously manicured gardens, stunning pools, a fitness club and more facials/massages/treatments than you could ever cope with, this spa offers the ultimate indulgence in Miami.

Taking a group yoga or meditation class is also a great way to relax and revitalize, most especially when you happen to be in one of Miami's very best studios.

The Standard Integrated Wellness

Revitalize your body, mind and spirit at The Standard, where classes, seminars and treatments offer a very holistic and comprehensive experience. From acupuncture to didgeridoo classes, meditation and hypnosis, the relaxing, invigorating and enlightening program at The Standard is heaven-sent.

Chapter 8: Feast like a local

Feasting whilst on vacation is an imperative must-do and never is this credo taken more seriously than in Miami. Even locals aren't exempt! Renowned for the sheer variety of fare on offer, and the above-average quality of meals, Miami is a kick-ass foodie destination for any ravenous woman. Whether you want to grab a quick bite seaside, or plan to splurge on one of the city's hottest eateries, there's never any reason to settle for an 'average' meal in Miami.

Here are our top picks:

Cheap & Cheerful

100 Montaditos – You probably wouldn't expect to get a delightful snack for $1 ANYWHERE, but at Montaditos it's precisely what you'll score for delectable mini-baguettes filled with chorizo, Serrano ham, melt-in-your mouth cheeses and lots more. The

taste of Spain with the price of Thailand – what more could one woman want? Branches are in Downtown and Brickell. Head here on a Wednesday and every item on the menu is just $1. Buen provecho!

Daily Bread Marketplace - Give us today our daily bread...or so the story goes. At Daily Bread you can indulge in a delicious platter of Middle Eastern delights, like pumpkin-spiced hummus, falafel, tabouli and grilled pita for under $10. Include in that a sinful serve of honey-drenched baklava. Alhamdulillah! You'll find these guys on SW 27th street and, before you come, don't forget to check out their FB page for daily specials.

Joe's Stone Crab – When Miami-ites think of fried chicken, they think of Joe's Stone Crab, funnily enough. This Miami Beach icon is mostly revered for its stone crab platters and although this will not be the cheapest meal in Miami, their fried chicken surely fits the bill. At one of the beach's best eateries you can order a half fried chicken for $7 which, in our books, constitutes a very cheap and cheerful lunch indeed. This price has not changed in two decades. Keep this spot in mind for a very worthy crabby splurge!

Jamaica Kitchen – For a Caribbean taste with all the trimmings head to this small but well stocked grocery store and café on SW 72nd Street. Grab a stool, drool at the menu on the wall and feast away. Here, you have a choice of beef, chicken or fish platters, which all come with a side serve of fried plantains and rice. Prices range from $8 to $12 depending on your protein of choice, and note that servings are very generous.

Josh's Deli – When nothing tickles your taste buds more than a delicious smoked pastrami on rye, then it's time to head to Josh's. Hand-smoked, home-pickled and freshly baked, the delights at Josh's aren't just incredibly good, they're also incredibly cheap. For under $15 Josh will teach you that not all sandwiches are boring, and not all are created equal. You'll find Josh feeding countless customers, on Harding Ave.

La Sandwicherie – Continuing on this outstanding sandwich theme, we present you La Sandwicherie, the favored alcohol-absorption venue of all proud Miami party goers. To be fair, they could fill their French baguettes with cardboard, and as long as they topped it with their amaaaazeballs vinaigrette dressing, everyone would still come back for seconds. Cured hams, melting cheeses and just enough salads to make you feel all healthy, the treats here are just phenomenal. La Sandwicherie has two branches: 14th Street and SW 8th.

La Camaronera – Die and go to Cuba at this delightfully small seafood haven in Little Havana. Elbow your way through this hole in the wall and we guarantee you'll emerge a totally different woman. By the time you've devoured perfectly fried lobster and shrimp, even your Spanish will have improved. Prometemos!

72

<u>Yakko-San</u> – Affordable Japanese? Is there really such a thing? In Miami, the answer is a resounding yes! One of Miami's best eateries, Yakko-San may not be the cheapest of the lot, but is certainly one of the best and, if you're a woman who prefers quality over quantity then it can certainly be a very inexpensive feed. Their bar bites are just $5 each and will make your taste buds jump for joy.

Best brunch

Most discerning women will agree: the best brunches are boozy and plentiful. In Miami...your wish is most definitely their command.

<u>Cecconi's</u> – Feast, see and be seen at this Miami institution, although prying away your eyes from your plate may be a bit of a challenge. People-watching may just have to wait. Grab a garden table, dive into the buffet brimming with insanely delicious pasta, pancakes, pizza, steaks, seafood and sweets – and

don't forget to swing by the omelet station – and wash it all down with a Bellini. Voila'. Brunch perfection.

Batch Gastropub – If the bottomless jug of sangria for $20 won't convince you that this is the best value-for-money brunch in Miami, then the cornbread eggs Benedict and drunken French toast surely will.

Hakkasan – Have a dim sum indulgence the way it's meant to be: fast, fresh and fery delicious. This may not be the cheapest Chinese treat you can have in Miami, but it is one of the best, so definitely worth the extra cash for a worthwhile brunch. With a great ambience and good reputation (the London Hakkasan is even Michelin starred) this is truly a gorgeous brunching experience. The dim sum lunch is only offered on weekends.

Oliver's Bistro – Oliver's ticks off quite a few boxes, with excellent service and consistently great food being just two. The gorgeous outdoor terrace is loved by locals who not only flock here in droves, but are also quite keen to keep the secret under wraps. Unravel the delicious menu and feast on salads, eggs any-way-you-like, fresh salmon and home-baked bagels, all complemented by heavenly mimosas.

Tongue & Cheek – the latest addition to the Miami brunch scene has taken the city by storm. The exceptional beef cheek burger may be to blame. Find unusual brunch items, alongside more classic fare like huevos rancheros, on the very creative menu at this über-trendy spot on Washington Avenue.

Trendiest restaurants

Of all the categories, this is perhaps the most difficult to pin down. Trend is not only a very relative term, but also a very transient one, in Miami particularly. Eateries can open and close at the blink of an eye, what's in today may well be out tomorrow and the place to be seen this week was probably not even open a month ago. That's just Miami for you. Nevertheless, there are a few staples which seem to consistently keep the quality of their fare top-notch, and their popularity equally soaring. Here are our faves:

Azul – Azul is an absolute hottie in every sense. With its eclectic fusion menu, great décor and swanky atmosphere, it's swiftly become the 'it' place to dine, even though it really hasn't been open all that long. The fact that it's the leading restaurant of the Mandarin Oriental Hotel, however, is indicative of the fact that it's probably not going anywhere, anytime soon. So if you like your beef to be Angus, your crabs King and service impeccable, this is the fine-dining option for you.

Centro Taco – Considering this is the brainchild behind another two of Miami's best restaurants, it's fair to assume the initial hype is more than just…well…hype. Good ol' Florida fare with a most definite Mexican infusion (Florida alligator tacos, anyone?) Centro Taco is all about quality. Tacos are made fresh to order and filled with all sorts of mouthwatering fillings.

Eating House — this Coral Gables institution hasn't really been open long enough for it to attain cult status, but that's precisely what it has achieved. The food is varyingly rated as 'outrageously delicious' and 'inconceivably good' and we don't think they are all exaggeration. With a concise and oft changed menu, the emphasis here is on the crème de la crème of local produce. Only the freshest and best ingredients, end of. The chicken waffles, carbonara and rock shrimp are the star attractions.

Ergon Greek Deli — Say you're with your girlfriends in Miami, it's your last night in town and you just wish to have a quiet night in together, chatting and sharing bubblies on the balcony of your seaside rental apartment. Where do you order dinner from?? From Ergon, of course! Bea local in the know, pop down to Coconut Grove and fill your suitcase — a picnic basket just won't do — with the best and most drool-worthy delicacies to have come out of Greece. Ever. Think feta cheese, steaming hot moussaka, garlicky gyros, spanakopita (spinach pies) and a host of other goodies. Eat in, take away and delivery are all available here. *Oppa!*

Lung Yai Thai Tapas – What do you get when you mix the flavors of Thailand and cuisine culture of Spain? Thai tapas, of course! Devour as much or as little as you like at this super trendy hot-spot, where Thai-inspired tapas are served till late every weeknight and very late on weekends.

Chapter 9: Shop 'till you drop

If it exists, you can buy it in Miami. Probably in the most unassuming shop you could ever imagine.

Shopping in Miami is totally fun, and not only because you can literally get anything you fancy here, but because unlike most other cities, there's just no order to the madness. In true Cuban style, perhaps, everything is everywhere; no 'genre' is clustered and just because you find a haute couture boutique, don't simply assume it'll have haute couture boutiques flanking its side. In Miami, it'll probably have a $2 T-shirt shop on the left and hamburger take-away shop on the right. The great thing about this is that multitasking women will never get bored and, more importantly, never have to choose. Shall I go designer today or cheap and trendy? In Miami, you can buy it all on *one* shopping trip to just *one* location.

Miami's just cool that way.

Tropicana Flea Market

Buy food, clothing, hand-made jewelry, lamp shades and a couple of kittens at this market and you're all set. Two hundred stalls – some indoor, others outdoor – have been congregating here on weekends for over 30 years. This market's open from 7 am to 7 pm, Friday, Saturday and Sunday. When we said 'if it exists, you can buy it in Miami', we actually mean 'at this flea market'. Go famished.

Lincoln Road Mall

Lincoln Road is the epitome Miami shopping experienced, where fashionistas with limitless credit cards rub shoulders with European backpackers looking for cheap bikinis. While the emphasis is very much on trend and luxe, there are plenty of alternative and eclectic shops to keep the crowds equally mixed. With lots of dining options to boot, this stretch of pedestrian retail therapy haven is a one-stop-wonder for all.

Ocean Drive

This is Miami's 'to be experienced' spot even though – just between us – it may well be the worst shopping haunt of all. Everything is a tad overpriced and, given the crowds, it can also get a little annoying trying to get any serious shopping done. Nevertheless, strolling and window-shopping on Ocean Drive is a Miami-must, and if you happen to fall in love with something you see on a window display, then paying a few extra dollars for it won't be much of an issue.

Collins Avenue

Much like Lincoln Street Mall, Collins Avenue also has it all, including shoppers donning bikinis and designer sarongs. Figures. On Collins Avenue, you'll still find your Ralph Lauren, Zara, Mango and Banana Republic, but you'll also find lots of one-off boutique selling gorgeous gear at 'normal people' prices. Sometimes.

Dolphin Mall

Thank the retail gods that this mega outlet mall is *so* good, because hiking up 20 miles west of Downtown is no mean feat. You'll find way over 200 stores here, selling everything your heart could possibly desire, most of it at great outlet prices. This is Miami county's second-largest mall and boasts a huge cinema complex and is divided in three sections: playa, ramblas and moda. If you're looking for a shopping excursion akin to a full-day out, then the Dolphin Mall's he place to head to.

Antique Mall Y'All

In Palmetto Bay is where you'll find Miami's largest antique mall, and let us tell you this place is infinitely more enticing than it sounds. Chock-full of wonderful treasures, from homewares to collectibles, clothing, jewels and accessories, Antique Mall is a treasure trove of wonderful and very unique stuff, ideal for all stylish women, not just antique-lovers. Yes, it's cluttered and overwhelming at first, but sorting your way through the piles and hidden corners is half the fun.

Design District

Miami's Design District breaks from the usual mold here and is entirely dedicated to upscale shopping, so if that's what you're after – and wish to not waste time – then it'll be right up your designer-alley. From Bvlgari to Prada, Armani and Rolex, to top-class homewares and home décor ideas, you'll find the best of Miami right here. Plenty of trendy cafés, restaurants and clubs to keep you engaged for a whole day – and night.

Miami Fair-trade Marketplace

The motto of this marketplace is 'trade, not aid' and it's a mighty great one at that. If you're looking for some gorgeous and unique souvenirs, and wish to contribute to an amazing cause, than this Fair-trade marketplace is for you. At this Coral Gables market you'll find hand-made treats, from developing countries the world over, created by artisans who are assured of a good wage and humane living and working conditions. And isn't that something worth shopping for? From Peruvian earrings to Indian kaftans and wind chimes, Philippine glass-beaded necklaces and Honduran ceramics, you can literally 'shop around the world' under one roof, and feel very good about it all.

Miracle Mile

Coral Gable's main shopping drag is true testament of the suburb's elite essence. Stylish, European-inspired architecture vie for your attention, alongside hundreds of simply stunning boutiques. They say the eye often has to have its part, and at the Miracle Mile, it certainly does. Here, you find art galleries, theatres, restaurants, shops, shops and more shops, as well as beauty salons, florists and then some more.

Little Havana

Yes, you'll find Cuban cigars and rum on sale everywhere in Miami, for that all-encompassing Cuban shopping experience, you must head to Little Havana. Sure, some of the shops on Calle Ocho are kitsch and touristy, but even if you're not kitsch, you *are* a tourist, so may as well shop like one!

Insider tip for a top shopping experience

Just because everything ever made is on sale in Miami, it really doesn't mean you need to buy it, or even waste your precious vacation time window-shopping for it. Need a new bra? Miami, in fact, may not be the best place for that!

Leave the 'usual suspects' shop for when you're at home and, when visiting Miami, bring home something utterly unique.

From Florida map-shaped chopping boards to Miami skyline mobile cases and colorful pillow cases, the city is actually awash with Miami-dedicated souvenirs. On the corner of Lincoln and Collins is where you'll also find a few of those kitsch souvenir shops, where fun and inexpensive stocking fillers, and gag gifts, are super easy to find. You can scour down the Washington end of Lincoln as well, for more fun souvenirs.

Bikinis, sarongs and anything remotely related to 'beach outings' are all excellent Miami souvenirs, as is a deep tan and a new, lighter hairdo with LOTS of volume!

Chapter 10: Miami by night

Take it from us: you'll need very little help finding nightclubs and groovy late-night bars in Miami. Along the seaside, they're a dime a dozen.

Want to know what else you can do of an evening in Miami?

Take a look...

Late night shopping

Considering the heat of daytime Miami, going shopping at night is actually a phenomenal way to buy two birds with one stone. On the main tourist drags, you'll find stores open till late, so you can people watch, dine and shop, all at the same time!

Sunset yoga

Join the throngs of equally zen locals for a 6 pm yoga class at Bayfront Park, and your evening will start off in the most relaxing of ways.

87

Play Bingo at The Standard

Sound too old fashioned for you? Think again! Once you've had an amazing pampering at the Standard's spa, you won't need much convincing that this is one of Miami's most in-the-know spots. Head here on Sunday nights and play bingo with locals, for your fun chance to win yet another amazing spa treatment, or free hotel stay! Grab a cocktail, enjoy the view and don't forget to tick off those numbers.

Open air cinema

Fancy a film with a stunning backdrop? Then Miami's open-air cinema's got you covered. Movies Under the Stars is an amazing evening activity, and in Miami you have different movie genres and locations to choose from. Foreign films are at the Hollywood Anniversary Park, classics at Huizenga Plaza and the ultimate 'drive-in' experience can be enjoyed in Fort Lauderdale.

Evening boat ride

Miami's cityscape is renowned for being drop-dead gorgeous, yet seen at night, from the water, it is more than spectacular. You'll find a plethora of cruise agencies offering sunset champagne boat rides (Miami Aquatours included) and this is, by far, the most magical way to spend the first few hours of your evening.

Night tour

Perhaps you want to do more than just cruise around. To this end, join an evening tour of the ArtDeco district, and cap it off with a superlative dinner *and* a cruise. Check out the details here.

Have a laugh

Whether alone or with a bunch of girlfriends, a night out in Miami's best comedy improv club is an absolute blast. Head to the Just the Funny Theatre and spend just $10 per person for a great couple hours of fab entertainment.

Jazz it up

Le Chat Noir is a hidden Downtown gem, ideal for lovers of cool, dark little live jazz venues. The cheese, charcuterie and wine on offer are a great incentive to *really* appreciate good jazz.

Catch a theatre show

Miami's performing art scene is quite impressive, considering the city is renowned as more of a show-offy, even superficial kind of hub. If you're keen to catch a show, be it ballet, a play, musical or concert, you'll probably find it playing here during your visit. Check out this online guide to see what's on.

Clubbing and partying

Well, it's not like we could completely neglect this most iconic side of Miami, could we?

The key in Miami is to find the 'in and happening' place, at the time of your visit and, perhaps more importantly for classy ladies, to find a place not overrun by over-testosteroned lotharios. That's always nice.

Here are the classiest, best and most popular clubs and lounges in Miami:

The Sunset Lounge @ Mondrian Hotel — Whimsical, elegant, posh and sexy, this seaside lounge is divine in every way. This is one of the hottest lounges in town and, thanks to the not-inexpensive drinks list, it attracts a certain kind of upscale crowd.

Hoy Como Ayer — Dance salsa with the pros at this Little Havana institution, a fantastic club which fuses hypnotic Cuban culture and music in vibrant fashion.

Nikki Beach Club — If you're going to do a beach club of an evening, may as well make it the most popular. Nikki's is the place to head to, if you want to see the sculpted, pulled, toned and tanned of Miami Beach, with their clothes on. Sort of.

Liv @ Fontainebleau – The hotel that's been attracting the rich, famous and infamous for decades, Fontainebleau boasts a lobby that's seen more star-studded appearances than the Oscars, and that's no joke. Liv is the name of the in-house club and 'in' was a term coined in honor of it, we are quite sure. Dress to kill, hide your credit card in your bra and don't lose your marbles when you spot a celebrity. Go for it!

Clevelander - Right on Ocean Drive is where you'll stumble upon the epitome SoBe club: open, rooftop, sexy, hot and quite wild on occasions. The rooftop bar of the popular Clevelander Hotel offers dancing under the stars, scrumptious cocktails and an equally delicious crowd.

Chapter 11: Useful references

Official Vacation Guide: Lots of very useful info to plan your itinerary.

Weather in Miami: You think the weather is predictable in tropical Miami, but you could be wrong. Better check!

Miami Herald and Miami Today: For the latest local news.

Swoop: Fun and creative way to get to know South Beach with locals.

Foreign Consulates: A list of consulates and embassies in Miami, in case you're travelling from abroad.

Miami Beach parking: Plan on driving? Here's where you can park.

AirBnB: Rent a room or a whole villa, directly from homeowners in Miami.

Campsites: Backing around Florida and wish to camp? Here's where you can pitch your tent or park your RV.

Disability Guide: Have mobility issues? This guide can help.

TripAdvisor: For the very latest reviews on activities, attractions, restaurants, bars and tours.

"FLORENCE FOR WOMEN: THE ULTIMATE TRAVEL GUIDE FOR WOMEN"
by Erica Stewart

Excerpt from the first 2 Chapters

History and Culture

Any Florence travel guide can never be complete without detailing its rich history and culture. Our guide might specifically cater to our female readers, but it's still important to understand the area's history and culture, isn't it?

The history of Florence can be traced all the way back to the Etruscan times. The city was then known as Fiesole, one that dominated the entire region and was one of the most important Etruscan centers. As the Romans prepared for their war against Fiesole, they set up camp by the Arno River in the 1st century BC. This area was later called Florentia, which can roughly be translated to "destined to flower". Florence somehow managed to survive the Middle Ages as well, and soon became one of the most important cities on the planet.

Florence's growth suffered a major setback because of a dispute between the Ghibellines, those loyal to Emperor Frederick II, and the Guelfs, those loyal to the pope. This led to the Guelfs being exiled from the city, but their absence was apparently short-lived, for they took over Florence once the Emperor succumbed to his death. Despite all the political turmoil, great attention was paid to arts and architecture, and this is one of the main reasons why Florence stands like a shining architectural jewel and a stark reminder of the romantic architectural wonders of a bygone era.

Art and culture were integral to the way of life as well. The desire of its locals to educate themselves led to the birth of the first works in the vernacular language in the form of "Dolce stil novo". This later inspired countless artists such as Boccaccio, Dante and Petrarca as well. In fact, Boccaccio's documentation of the Florence plague is one of the most accurate descriptions of a tragedy that began as dissatisfaction and ended with the "Tumulto dei Ciompi" in the year 1378.

Florence saw a small period where the people took over the rule of the city. However, this was evidently short-lived as the Medici dynasty soon took over. The Medici emperor Lorenzo il Magnifico was also responsible for much of the city's wonderful Brunelleschi architecture. After his death in the year 1492, the city once again fell into turmoil, but this era of conflict still managed to see the rise of world famous artists such as Leonardo da Vinci and Michelangelo.

From the 18th century up until the very beginning of the 20th century, Florence remained famous for its literary offerings and artistic wonders. It produced some of the best works of literature created by writers such as Palazzeschi, Papini and Pratolini, all of whom were members of the literary group "Giubbe Rosse".

Getting There and Around

Florence is well-connected to the rest of Europe and is easy to get into. It has witnessed a drastic increase in tourism over the past few years, and this has led to the development of all sorts of high-tech facilities and traveler-friendly infrastructure.

Getting There

The best way to travel to Florence is by air. The Aeroporto Firenze-Peretola is the main airport of Florence and is located at a distance of 2.5 miles from the city center. The ideal way to commute from the airport is to board the shuttle bus which connects the airport to the Santa Maria Novella station and runs at intervals of 30 minutes between 06.00AM and 11.40PM. Taxi services are available as well.

Getting Around

It makes sense to leave your cars behind while traveling to Florence. And even if you're coming from a faraway destination, forget all about that car rental. As women, one of our main concerns is our security, particularly when traveling to different countries. However, when it comes to Florence, you really don't need a car for most of its major attractions are located in its historic city center, an area best explored on foot (vehicles aren't allowed to enter the city center without prior authorization either). And visiting other destinations is easy as well, for Florence boasts of a decent public transportation system that lets you get from point A to point B without much fuss.

I recommend using the taxi services while in the city, particularly if you're traveling alone. Florence taxis are white in color and can be picked up from a taxi rank or be booked on the phone. Taxi ranks can easily be found in front of the main plazas and railway stations. Some of the top taxi operators in Florence include SO.CO.TA (+39 055 4242) and CO.TA.FI (+39 055 4390).

Florence is relatively small, and this means that a woman can really have a blast while exploring its streets on a bike. There are a number of cycle tracks in the city as well, and this certainly makes things easier. Some of the top bike rental companies to hire your bikes from include Alinari (+39 055 280500), Rentway (+333 9619820), and Florence by bike (+39 055 488992).

For women who like to keep it adventurous, the Segway offers a fascinating option of getting from one place to the other. It's convenient, it's simple and it's certainly super exciting. You can book your Segways by calling +39 055 2398855.

Finally, it is very hard to resist the romantic feel of riding in an open carriage. These enchanting rides transport you to a bygone era and Florence's enchanting cobblestone streets offer the perfect backdrop to relive yesterday. You can easily pick up a carriage in Piazza San Giovanni, Piazza Duomo and Piazza della Signoria.

Staying in Florence

Florence is one of the top cities in Italy for any woman wanting to choose from a wide range of safe, secure, exciting and inviting accommodations. Florence was among the first cities in Italy to develop its hotel scene, particularly because of the efforts of local designer Michele Bonan, who has now left his mark on hotels across the country, and the hospitality division of the Ferragamo Group, Lungarno Hotels.

Hotels for Every Budget

The city has always enjoyed a great tradition of hospitality and she takes a lot of pride in introducing her female travelers to some of its best-kept secrets. There's a lot of choice across all budgets, even in the historic city center, the place where you really want to be. Better yet, the competition amongst hotels keeps rates at a low, particularly during the off season.

For Ladies Wanting to Live like Locals

If you're dreaming of staying in an area that is full of artisan workshops, real people and hidden cafes, look no further than the Oltrarano district. Some of the top accommodation options include the cute B&B Floroom 1 and the Palazzo Magnani Feroni.

Billed as one of the top bed and breakfasts in the city, **B&B Floroom 1** is a sleek address located on the banks of the Arno River, and one of the top choices for solo female travelers looking for budgeted options in the city. This four-bedroom B&B boasts of an extremely relaxed atmosphere and each of its four rooms feature wooden floors, white walls, rustic ceilings and giant photographs of Florence. The old-new combination works quite well and really makes the property stand out. Some rooms also boast of four-poster beds, and an opaque glass wall hides away the comfy bathroom that has been fitted with pewter fittings and rainforest showerheads.

The **Palazzo Magnani Feroni** is one hotel that you'd never want to leave. It makes you feel like the nobility of yesterday and transports you to a historic location that makes you forget about everything else. Each aristocratic suite boasts of beautiful high curved ceilings and heirloom furniture and the terrace views rank among the very best.

For the Budget-Conscious Woman (Medium Range)

Casa Di Barbano is a simple option that offers great value for money. It is spacious and elegant and its owners are extremely friendly. All rooms are comfortable to say the least, and when you factor in the convenient location, safe accommodations, and reasonable costs, you have everything you need to explore Florence like a pro.

Casa Nuestra is one of the hippest addresses in the city. This brand new B&B is located close to the Campo di Marti station, and is characterized by its super friendly hosts. Apart from offering picture-perfect accommodations, the owners also go out of their way to assist you in planning your itineraries, show you how to explore the city and help you uncover enchanting walking paths.

For the Lady Who Travels in Style…. (Luxury)

Palazzo Vecchietti is one of the most elegant and beautiful hotels in the city. This boutique hotel boasts of stylish rooms, easy access to Via Tornabuoni and a superior level of service. The furnishings have been tastefully appointed, and great attention has been paid to every detail. Beds are comfy and usually include quality beddings and cashmere blankets. They are the just about the perfect places to snuggle into after a long and tiring day exploring the artistic wonders around the city.

Another popular option is the *St. Regis Hotel*. It boasts of a unique ambience that is both delightful and discreet at the same time. The hotel is located on an enchanting riverside location in centro storico and its Arno views appeals to female travelers who are accustomed to the highest standards of pampering. The service is warm and welcoming, professional and casual, discreet and attentive. Everything you'd want it to be. And the rooms are just what you'd expect from a hotel like St. Regis. I would recommend the Bottega Veneta suite, a top option for fashion-conscious women.

Things to See and Do

No matter how many times you come to visit this iconic beauty, you won't be able to see it all. A bridge on the Arno River is one of the first destinations that you should visit while in Florence. It is known to offer different experiences at different times of the day, for the views, the light, and the atmosphere changes each and every time. Considered to be the birthplace of the Renaissance, Florence also boasts of some of the best art and architecture in history. No wonder it manages to draw millions of tourists year after year.

Walking in the Footsteps of Michelangelo

Very few artists have managed to leave their mark on a city the way Michelangelo has in Florence. The city is home to some of his greatest masterpieces, and one of the biggest charms of visiting the city is to retrace his steps and explore places that are linked to his memories. Embarking on the following itinerary not only lets you retrace Michelangelo's steps, but also brings you closer to some of the most important arts and monuments in Florence. Remember, the ideal way to make the most of this itinerary is to spread it over two days, so that you get enough time to marvel at the various wonders and enjoy all that it has in store for you.

Start off your explorations at the *Casa Buonarroti*. Located in the vibrant Santa Croce, Casa Buonarroti is the palace where the artist's family lived. It was built by his nephew Leonardo, and passed hands from one member of the family to another until the iconic family finally became extinct. Casa Buonarroti hosts some of the earliest works of

Michelangelo such as the *Madonna della Scala* and the *Battle of the Centaurs*. The former is a tribute to sculptor Donatello while the latter has been inspired by the Garden of San Marco. Both masterpieces were created by the artist while he was in his twenties, and imagining a young boy creating such outstanding works of art is an exciting experience in itself.

The next destination is the **Church of Santo Spirito**, another place that has been intricately linked with Michelangelo during his early days. Located in the Oltrarno district, the church is considered to be one of the most beautiful Renaissance-era churches on the planet. It was also the place where Michelangelo found accommodation after his patron Lorenzo de Medici died in the year 1492. The church is famous for its inspiring wooden *Crucifix* that Michelangelo created in the year 1493.

The next step of your journey takes you to the **Bargello Museum**. Michelangelo was forced to move to Rome in the year 1494 after the city riots sent Medici into exile, and it was in Rome that he created the world famous *Bacchus*, now located in the Bargello Museum. The museum is also home to other popular artworks created by the artist such as *David/ Apollo, Brutus,* and *Tondo Pitti*.

Don't forget to add the **Accademia Gallery** into your itinerary as well. Once Michelangelo returned to Florence in the year 1501, he set about creating some of his best works of art, including the outstanding *David*, now located in the Accademia Gallery. The Accademia is also home to many of his unfinished figures and sculptures. From the *"non finito"* sculpting techniques of *St. Mathew* to the marble wonder *Prigioni*, the Accademia truly showcases some of the most the distinct features of Michelangelo's style.

Head over to the **Uffizi Art Gallery** next. Considered to be one of the most famous art galleries in the world, Uffizi features a large collection of artworks created between the 12th and 17th centuries by leading artists such as Leonardo da Vinci, Botticelli, Raffaello and Giotto. The gallery also houses the *Tondo Doni*, Michelangelo's first canvas painting and the only of its kind in Florence.

Between the years 1515 and 1534, the Medici family saw two of its members becoming popes – Clement VIII and Leo X. Michelangelo was commissioned to create the *Laurentian Library* for the *Basilica of San Lorenzo* and the *Sagrestia Nuova* for the **Medici Chapels**. Both works of art are a must see and the entire complex is also worth a visit for its artistic ingenuity.

The last Michelangelo masterpiece that you should admire during your stay in Florence is the *Pieta Bandini*. This dramatic work of art was created in the year 1550 and is now located in the **Museo dell'Opera del Duomo**. It is considered to be one of the greatest examples of the master's work and what makes it even more special is his self-portrait, a male figure flanked by Mary and Magdalene, holding the lifeless body of Christ.

Best Neighborhoods

When planning any vacation, one of the biggest concerns for women is to choose the right neighborhood. There are some areas that have traditionally been famous for being safe for women, while ensuring that they don't miss out on the very best of nightlife and cosmopolitan delights that the city has to offer. When it comes to Florence, you need to decide between three choices – staying in the historic center, staying outside of the historic center or staying in the surrounding countryside. All three areas have safe neighborhoods for women, so it ultimately boils down to personal preference. Here are a few options to choose from.

Staying Within the Historic Center

The city center always dominates a major part of your holiday for most of the historic sights and attractions are located here. The area is among the oldest parts of the city, and the ring that you see is basically the spot where those 13th century walls were built. The city center is quite small, and car free as well. This means that you can easily walk from one place to the other and not miss a car throughout your journey. Staying close to the Santa Maria Novella station puts you within a 5-minute walk from the Duomo and staying close to the Duomo pits you within a 5-minute walk from Ponte Vecchio and Palazzo Vecchio. The ideal way to choose an area is to look for accommodations close to the sites you really like. Since most of the major sites are quite close to each other, I suggest staying between Piazza Santa Croce, Piazza San Marco, Piazza Santa Maria Novella and Pont Vecchio. This area is among the busiest areas in the city and is always full of tourists all through the day and in the evenings as well. The second option is to look for accommodations in the Oltrarno neighborhood, but that only works if you're leaning towards local experiences, unique furniture galleries and the Pitti Palace.

Staying Outside the Historic Center

With most of the restaurants, cafes, sights and attractions located within the historic center, you would argue if it makes sense to stay outside the center. However, many female travelers visiting Florence end up booking accommodations outside its historic center for all sorts of reasons. The biggest advantage of staying outside the city center is that it is friendlier on the wallet. Moreover, anyone wanting to stay in a residential area to explore the local way of life needs to step outside the touristic city center. A few areas that aren't really far from the main sights of the city include Via Bolognese, Fortezza da Basso, Poggio Imperiale and Piazza Beccaria.

Staying in the Surrounding Countryside

If you're thinking of keeping Florence as a base for exploring Tuscany, you might want to head over to the surrounding hills. Apart from letting you get up close and personal to nature, it also lets you enjoy all sorts of amenities such as gardens, outdoor areas and swimming pools in your accommodations without forcing you to pay through the roof. Having your own rental car is a must while staying in the outskirts, but it's perfect for exploring Tuscany to its fullest.

THE END